Spiritual Inspirations:

SACRED WORDS OF WISDOM

Ann Marie Ruby

DEDICATION

I have dedicated each one of my books to the person or people whom have inspired me to write the soul of the book. I would like to dedicate this book not to a person, but an inspiration that I have carried throughout my life. All the authors in this world are but inspired for different reasons, but we all use as a gift to bring these books upon your hands, the best friend of an author, words.

Words are sacred and have been used wisely by the past to the present throughout the future. I believe that even though humans are but mortal, words live on forever. The wind whispers sweet songs throughout time as she sings throughout eternity, her eternal friend, words. A mother sings her child to sleep with her eternal friend, words. A teacher blesses all throughout history, as she asks for help from her friend, I call words.

I have written this book and all my books holding on to the powerful hands of my friend, I call words. For this, I dedicate my book, *Spiritual Inspirations: Sacred Words Of Wisdom*, to the most blessed inspiration we all have as we travel throughout life, words.

INTRODUCTION

Spiritual inspiration comes from within the soul. All of us throughout this journey of life have something that inspires us to awaken from within ourselves. My inspiration was, is, and shall always be words. Life is a gift we live and share, within all different race, culture, and religion.

The sky, our roof, the Earth, and our foundation we share amongst each other. The only sacred spiritual connection we have between each other is words. Words travel time to guide us throughout eternity. From the past to the present throughout the future, words remain as our spiritual inspiration.

From the souls of the wise, to the souls of all whom but seek solace, words remain like a guide. I have taken this friend, I call words, as my guide throughout my spiritual journey of life. Eternally, I walk only to inspire all throughout eternity.

In this book, I have my original quotations from within my walk of life. As I have traveled life, I have gathered my inspiration into words. Life is a blessed teacher for all of us, the creation. As we walk, we learn and gather more information along the way. I call all of these, *Spiritual Inspirations: Sacred Words Of Wisdom*, as we travel through life.

May my quotations be of inspiration to all of you throughout your journey of life. All sacred travelers, may you find upon your travel throughout life, my Spiritual Collection. May she be a friend, a helping hand, who shall always be there throughout the lonely nights, the troubled times, and even throughout the blessed times. May my books be there for you today and the future tomorrow. With all my blessings, I give you from my Spiritual Collection, this book I have named, *Spiritual Inspirations: Sacred Words Of Wisdom.*

MESSAGE FROM THE AUTHOR

Time passes by leaving behind blessings from the words of wisdom. Words are but a sacred grace left upon us throughout history. Holding on to them ever so gently, we walk towards the future. Within the embrace of spirituality, we but awaken. Inspiration, I find for everything in my life comes from the pure wisdom of spirituality, devotion, and meditation.

I gently keep within my soul, all the blessings of spirituality and words of inspiration. For this reason, I write spiritual quotations, and spiritual songs I call prayers. I know as time passes by and we all end upon the land of the past, we still have the gifts we leave behind throughout time.

My gift to the present, the future, and the past as time travels by us, is my inspirational words of wisdom. May my words awaken all humans and bless them with spiritual awakening, as we all must be the candles of hope for all generations to come.

May my words travel time and be an inspiration for all whom are but looking for the candles of hope. May I be the candle who shines throughout time and awakens within all, the blessings of humanity. Hold my hands and may you too be the candles of hope amongst all around you as we light all hearts within the blessings of spiritual inspiration and become the candles of hope throughout eternity.

For all spiritual souls looking for peace and blessings throughout the journey of life, I give you yet again another spiritual quotation book. I call her, *Spiritual Inspirations: Sacred Words Of Wisdom*.

THE WORDS OF MY LORD

My Lord, forgive.

My Lord, forgive.

My Lord, forgive.

Let these hands not sin.

Let these eyes not sin.

Let these lips not sin.

Let these ears not sin.

Let this mind, body, and soul not sin.

Let these feet not land upon sin.

My Lord, forgive.

My Lord, forgive.

My Lord, forgive.

When this mind, body, and soul

Reach land of sin,

My Lord, let me be protected within Your bounds.

Oh my Lord, hear my prayers.

Let this mind, body, and soul be awakened.

Oh my Lord, I live amongst sinners.

I live amongst sin.

I walk amongst sin.

Let me hold on to You

And be Your true, faithful devotee.

Let me be Yours and only Yours.

Let me find my way back to You.

Amongst the sinners I am,

But pure and sin free I am.

I stand upon the land of sin,

But I stand sin free.

I stand amongst the disbelievers,

But I am a believer.

I call upon You.

All around me, disbelievers walk.

I know of the truth,

But they are flooding me with their lies.

I know the truth,

But they are drowning me amongst their lies.

My heart knows You are there,

But their words are drowning me.

May I be strong.

May I have the courage to announce the truth

Amongst the disbelievers.

Alone I walk, frightened I am,

But on this journey I have my faith

And my love for my Lord and the truth,

The unknown, untold truth,

The veil The Lord has created

To separate Heaven and Earth.

I know I must walk for You, my Lord.

With this faith and love, I shall be strong.

I know my Lord is there when I fall.

I know my Lord is there

When I am but put down by the human.

Their sharp tongue and their knowledge of nothing

And their voice of wrong but shouts so loud.

I look at them walking and I know

Their empty vessels make so much noise

For I carry the love of my Lord.

I know this journey is hard,

But at the end, my Lord is there.

Oh my Lord, I ask of You not for anything,

But give me strength and wisdom,

And Your love, and courage.

Even alone, may I fight until my last breath.

When my breath is no more,

May my soul still fight

For the words I leave behind shall grow stronger,

Mouth to mouth, ears to ears.

My words shall take voice

And shall take form of humans

And multiply

And shall be

The words of my Lord.

The words of my Lord.

THE WORDS OF

MY LORD.

*From my prayer book, *Spiritual Songs: Letters From My Chest*.

"*Inspirations* are words of *wisdom* here to *guide* all. They have *traveled* through *the* journey of *time* and *endured* all the *obstacles*."

Quotation #1

"*From* dawn to dusk
and dusk to *dawn*,
we are but *never*
alone, *hands*
spread like
an *umbrella*,
The *Creator* is
always watching
over *us*."

Quotation #2

2

"*Hope* watches over all as she *takes* birth with *faith*."

Quotation #3

"*The* journey of life begins at *birth* and ends at *death*. May this *journey* be *forever* as we become a *page* in *history*."

Quotation #4

"*Do* not become the *critic* and knock upon *another* door, for *remember* the *pain* she had *caused* when she had but *knocked* upon your *door*."

Quotation #5

"*Dreams* are the sacred gifts of *life*. *Hold* on to them *sacredly*, for then through *dreams*, life will *become complete*."

Quotation #6

"*Love* is *immortal* even though *humans* are but mortal. *Love* lives on *beyond* time. She *travels* through *time* as she turns the *past* into *history*."

Quotation #7

"*Hold* on to the hands of *hope* as she is the only *path* to *victory*."

Quotation #8

"*Touch* all around you through *words*, for even *though words* are invisible, they *touch* where nothing else *can*."

Quotation #9

"*The* artist catches all different colors on her canvas for then the art is but complete. The Creator laid all different race, color, and religion, onto this Earth and this is how we become a part of the complete *picture.*"

Quotation #10

"*Do* not look for *eternity* and miss out on all the *blessings* of the *present.* *Accept* the present and *make* this day *eternal.*"

Quotation #11

"*For* inspiration, all you have to *do* is look into your *past* and see your *innocent past* watching over *you*."

Quotation #12

"*Hold* on to the *memories* of the past and *bring* back the *innocent* child within your *soul*. *Grow* up with dignity *and* courage, keeping the *innocent* childhood alive *all* throughout *time*."

Quotation #13

"*Life* is a
sacred journey where
all around we see what
our heart but desires.
A bright sunny day
desires love, joy,
and peace. A stormy
night holds on to
the memories of the
past. Throughout all,
life is a sacred
journey."

Quotation #14

"*When* in pain and sorrow, all around seem dark. The skies burst out all the tears. Today, throughout the summer nights of joy, and love, do not forget your past who but was in *pain*."

Quotation #15

"*Miracles* happen as we *hold* on to *humanity*. Hold on to each *other* as we *bring* back *humanity*."

Quotation #16

"*Hope* blooms throughout the *lands* like *wildflowers*. Be the one to *plant* the seeds of *hope* as she *awaits* your *blessings*."

Quotation #17

"*Bring* into
your life *patience*,
forgiveness,
blessings, *and* love.
Let this *ocean* of
virtues *flow* from your
soul to all whom
but *seek*."

Quotation #18

"*With* complete faith, hold on to the *spirits* of hope for *hope walks* back *spiritually* as she *awakens* all within the *blessings* of *hope*."

Quotation #19

"*Destiny* is but the complete *journey* of life. *Create* your own *destiny* as you *live* life *completely*."

Quotation #20

"*With* each
disappointment, *we*
walk closer to the
achievements of *life*.
May *you* endeavor
in all *aspects* of life
as you *cross*
the *bridge* of
disappointment."

Quotation #21

"*May* my words be *prayers* in the wind *blowing* peace *throughout* the world. *May* all *houses* have their *windows* open to let this wind of *peace* into their *homes* and *hearts*."

Quotation #23

"*Knocking*
on a door that has been closed, seeking for something that is invisible, asking for help from the stranger who pretends not to be there, is fruitless. Persistence is fruitful. Keep knocking, seeking, and asking, for with persistence, you shall but *prevail*."

Quotation #23

"*Words* are the true *healers* of all time. Spread *them* with love and *harmony* as they shall *carry* on to the *future* to *heal* all even throughout *time*."

Quotation #24

"*Forever*, words of *wisdom* remain in the *hearts* of whom she but has *touched*. This *bond* becomes *eternal* as words become the *sacred* journey of *wisdom*."

Quotation #25

"*Peace* brings forth upon all *creation* basic human *values*. Carry them *within* your *basket* of bread as you too give *birth* to *humanity*."

Quotation #26

"*Arrive* at the station of *peace* as you travel through *life*. This is the *only* stop *where* you will be in *peace* as you spread *peace*."

Quotation #27

"*Irritation* is the *thorn* between the devoted *and* devotion of the *devotee.*"

Quotation #28

"*Sleep* is the enemy of meditation, devotion, and awakening. For we are all but searching for the complete awakening of the mind, body, and soul, which is acquired through *knowledge.*"

Quotation #29

"*Gain* knowledge and be *awakened completely* through *spirituality* and let this *life* journey be the *complete awakening* of the *inner* mind, body, and *soul*."

Quotation #30

30

"*Accept* the truth and set free all the negativities of the mind, body, and soul. With all your love, hold on to all the positivity of this universe, for only then, you shall be free and awakened *spiritually*."

Quotation #31

"*Meditate* to
release the negative
energy and bring
all positivity to your
mind, body, and
soul. Negative energy
brings down the
mind, body, and soul,
while within positive
energy, all things
are but *achieved*."

Quotation #32

"*Love* what
you are doing, for it is
then, you will achieve
the positive results
your soul but seeks.
Do not seek to please
the others, but first
please your mind,
body, and soul, and
then the results shall
be. All is but pleased
for you are
the *pleased.*"

Quotation #33

"*Do* not pray because otherwise the *society* makes you into a *prey*. Do it *for* the complete inner *peace*, for *only* then, the *prayers* are but *answered*."

Quotation #34

"*Knowledge* is given to the *wise* not *to* use it against *wisdom*."

Quotation #35

"*Meditation* is the complete *miracle* of the mind, body, *and* soul. *Believe* in it and *let* the miracles *begin*."

Quotation #36

"*Bathe* in
the spiritual wisdom.
Never let physical or
emotional obstacles
put you down. Stand
up for your right
and cross over all
the hurdles of life
with positivity as
you awaken spiritually
from the *inside*."

Quotation #37

"*Blessings* pour from the Heavens above like sprinkles of rain. Keep an eye out for them through devotion and meditation. Remember to catch them within the spirits of eternal *blessings*."

Quotation #38

"*Dreams* are sacred messages *from* the *unknown*, asking us to *complete* this *sacred* journey of *life.*"

Quotation #39

"*Lantern*, I keep burning, *so* we the *creation* of this *universe* find our way back *home*."

Quotation #40

"*Combatting* all *negativity*, through our *positivity*, is the only *way* to *awaken* our inner *peace*."

Quotation #41

"*Humans* become the spiritual *Angels* of *peace*, when we work for *each other* not against each *other*."

Quotation #42

"*With* all things going *around*, it *seems* like hope is *just* that, a *glimmer* away, waiting to be *found*."

Quotation #43

"*Peace* takes birth as we find *hope* for her. Hope *holds* on to all *dreams* throughout *the* dark nights and *blooms* to *glory* as dawn breaks *open*."

Quotation #44

"*Believe* in the *dreams* for they are *guidance* given to you as we *lay* down our mind, body, *and* soul for the *night*."

Quotation #45

"*Never* give up on your *dreams*, for as you *believe* in *yourself* and your *dreams*, it is only then, *others* shall *follow*."

Quotation #46

"*Even* though now it is only a *dream*, soon your *dreams* shall be a *reality*."

Quotation #47

"*Miracles* happen around every *corner* of our *lives*. It is when we *accept* them as *just* that, a pure *miracle*, the *blessings* are but *found*."

Quotation #48

"*Power* and mystery are *the* companions of *words*. The most *powerful* and *mysterious companion* of all *humanity* is but *words*."

Quotation #49

"*Words* become *immortal* as they *travel* through the *highways* of life. *Even* though humans *travel* through the *same* highways, *humans* are but *mortal*."

Quotation #50

"*As* the darkest part of the night *passes* us *by*, it is then the *brightest* star comes *shining* through the *night's* sky, *blessing* dawn upon *us*."

Quotation #51

"*Life* is a journey from the *past* to the *present* through the *future*, where we *share* this one-way *highway* with all *different* race, color, and *religion*."

Quotation #52

"*Basic* moral values *do* not need a *religion* but *just* that, basic moral *values*."

Quotation #53

53

"*Songs* are the *sweetest* energy of life. They *bring* to *union* all race, color, and *religion*."

Quotation #54

"*Time* wasted is *never*, for let *all* the time wasted be a *lesson* learned for the *future*."

Quotation #55

"*Breathe* in the pure blessings of *dawn* throughout the *day* as she *progresses* towards *nightfall*."

Quotation #56

"*Even* during the dark nights, we have the glorious moon shining upon us like a guiding star, with so many of her friends showing their twinkling lights throughout the dark *nights*."

Quotation #57

"*Blessings* from *Heaven* come in different *forms*. Acknowledge *them* with *caution* for it is then *they* convert for *you* either into a *blessing* or a *curse*."

Quotation #58

"*The* mystical power of *words* *spreads* peace throughout *all* the hearts reached. *Keep* these *words* safe within your *hearts*, as you too *become* a part *of* this mystical *journey*."

Quotation #59

"*Today*, welcome peace, love, *and* harmony *into* your *heart* through the *simplest* way of *words*."

Quotation #60

"*We* are all related. *Even* though *different* we may be, but if the *world* starts to *crumble*, we will *hold* on to each *other* even though *strangers* we may *be*."

Quotation #61

"*Hold* on to your *dreams*, for *remember* as you but *awaken*, it is up to you to *follow* your *dreams* and convert *them* into *reality*."

Quotation #62

"*From* the beginning of *time*, *people* have tried to *decode dreams*. Take them as a peace *symbol*, as *guidance*, as *spiritual awakening*."

Quotation #63

"*Dreams* are given from the *Heavens* above *onto* all within the *Earth* beneath for *within* them lie the *miracles* of *eternity*."

Quotation #64

64

"*Forgiveness* is the only way to *freedom*. Accept it and *set* your *mind*, body, and soul *free*."

Quotation #65

"*Peace* lands upon
the *soul*
as *forgiveness*
is but *found.*"

Quotation #66

"*The* most sacred gift
this life but *embarks*
upon *us* is forgiveness.
Holding *on* to the
oars of *forgiveness*,
journey *through*
this *life*."

Quotation #67

"*Swim* through the *ocean* of obstacles to reach your *goal*. All is *achievable* with *hope* and *positivity*."

Quotation #68

"*Miracles* are found everywhere *there* is *hope*, faith, and belief. Hold *on* to hope, *faith*, and *belief*, and the *path* to miracles shall *be*."

Quotation #69

"*Celebrate* victory, but never *forget* defeat. *Victory* only appears *after* we respect *defeat*."

Quotation #70

"*Love* is eternal for love took her *first* breath *from* The *Creator* to the *creation* and became *immortal*."

Quotation #71

"*Do* not run after
immortality, for
you then *become*
lost in *eternity*.
Find *love*
for she *is* eternally
immortal."

Quotation #72

"*Even* after taking a *bath* in the *ocean* of sin, the believers *rise* and *awaken* above the waters sin *free*."

Quotation #73

"Life is a blessed spiritual *song* written *throughout* time, *recited* throughout *eternity."*

Quotation #74

"*May* my words
be the *windchimes*
singing inspirational
tunes to *awaken*
all *humans*
throughout
eternity."

Quotation #75

"*Open* the doors to your *heart* and watch *love* enter in all aspects of *life*."

Quotation #76

"*Faith* finds her way as we *open* the door for *her*."

Quotation #77

"*Words* become *wisdom* sent from the *wise*, as she time *travels* through the journey of *life*."

Quotation #78

"*Life* is but mortal as death is *immortal*, in *between* we travel *time*."

Quotation #79

"*Sacred* spiritual *teachings* are but *immortal* words whom *travel* throughout *time*."

Quotation #80

"*Travel* time through the *eyes* of the past, present, *and* the *future*, for then, even your *journey* is *written* as an *inspirational* guide throughout *time*."

Quotation #81

"*For* love, the world but is. Within *love*, all but is *found*. *May* we keep love within our *hearts*, for then *we* shall *have* all that is but *needed*."

Quotation #82

"*Within* the soul, *resides* the *knowledge* of the complete *truth*. *Turn* it on like the *lighthouse* in the *middle* of *nowhere*."

Quotation #83

"*Spiritual* awakening is like the *lantern* from within a *soul*, guiding *us* to *complete enlightenment* from *within*."

"*Hold* on to the *candles* of hope throughout the *dark* night's sky, for *dawn* peaks *through* the *windows* as she *awakens* all within *the* warmth of *hope*."

Quotation #85

85

"*The* human mind and *body* carry the *burdens* of life, as the human *soul* carries the *blessings* of the spiritual *soul*."

Quotation #86

"*Water* quenches the *physical* thirst, yet only *spiritual awakening quenches* the spiritual *soul*."

Quotation #87

"Life's eternal lessons are the *struggles* and *endeavors* we land *upon,* as we *journey* through this *life."*

Quotation #88

"*Troubled* times shall *pass* by like the *waves* of the *ocean*. Keep steady *and* stay *afloat* until you find *shore*."

Quotation #89

"*During* an inner spiritual *storm*, hold on to the *ark* of faith and *wisdom* to *overcome* this spiritual *storm*."

Quotation #90

"*Angels* walk amongst the *humans*. Do not *go* out *looking* for them, but become *one*."

Quotation #91

"*Teachers* are the spiritual healers of history. Take the first step and become the student for with time, history shall remember you as a *teacher*."

Quotation #92

"*History* only retells what *we* leave behind. Let us *make* history today, the *way* we want the *future* to remember *us*."

Quotation #93

"*The* past walks into the *present* as she *gifts* the future all the positivity of *life.*"

Quotation #94

"*Life* is an example of all the *lessons* one but lives and *leaves* behind. *Be* an *example* for all life to *come*."

Quotation #95

"*Fear* but takes away all positivity and becomes an obstacle of fear. Erase all the fears from the books of life, and walk with positivity as you rewrite your own book with hope, faith, and *positivity*."

Quotation #96

"*Hope* keeps brewing
in the ocean of *life*,
as she *travels*
from land to *land*,
washing all
with *hope*."

Quotation #97

"*War* brews
hate and destroys
all life around her.
Pour love
and blessings over
all hate and be
victorious as you
watch love grow
all around, creating
a sacred spiritual
life."

Quotation #98

"*Hold* on to the hands of *hope* even *when* she lets go, for then it is *you* who must *be* the hope and *inspiration* for *all* to follow and hold on *to*."

Quotation #99

"*Spiritual* inspiration *awakens the* mind, body, and soul. Even *when* all but fall *asleep,* spirituality *keeps* all *around* her *awakened* throughout *eternity.*"

Quotation #100

"*Time* is our only *spiritual* connection *from* the *past* to the present through the *future*. Value *time* as she will *carry* you from the *past* to the *present* through the *future*."

Quotation #101

"*Love* is life's eternal blessing. *Spread* love all *around* you and *find* life's eternal *blessing*."

Quotation #102

"*Peace* is always there *waiting* for your *invitation*. Invite her *over* to *dinner* tonight and be in *peace* forever *after*."

Quotation #103

"*Love* forever after, is *eternal.* Even when this *Earthy* vehicle *falls* asleep, love *lives* on forever *after.*"

Quotation #104

"*Do* not live *with* anger and *regret*. Let her go, set her *free*, and live within *peace* and *dignity*."

Quotation #105

"*Sprinkle* the
seeds of
love, joy, and hope,
as you continue
this journey of life,
for then the sun
shall shine upon the
future generation
with love, joy,
and *hope*."

Quotation #106

"*Keep* the candles *burning* for all of whom but need *hope*, for *then* you shall *find* yourself amongst all whom but *carry* the candles of *hope*."

Quotation #107

"*Music* creates a bond *between* the mind, body, *and* soul. Be the *music*, and create a *bond* between the *human* and *humanity*."

Quotation #108

"*A* knock from an *obstacle* awakens the *surviving* warrior *within* us. Knock *over* all the *obstacles* as you are *the* surviving *warrior*."

Quotation #109

"*Spirituality awakens* within the mind, body, *and* soul as all but *accept* her *within* the embrace of *peace* and *serenity.*"

Quotation #110

"*The* path to freedom is through *accepting* the blessings of *peace* and *harmony*. For it is *within* this *journey*, all souls are but *free*."

Quotation #111

"*Set* the teardrops free.
Do not *hold* her a
prisoner. For it
not only *hurts* her,
but drowns your soul
into the ocean of
sadness."

Quotation #112

"*Be* the lighthouse for all the lost *lovers* lost in the *ocean* of *tears*. Show them you were *there* once, but *now* have *become* the *lighthouse*."

Quotation #113

"*Spiritual* inspiration is *born* within the eternal love *of* each spiritually *inspired.* Be the *inspiration* as you *inspire* all *throughout* this journey of *life.*"

Quotation #114

"*Even* within the ocean of *sin*, be the *awakened* soul, the *eternal* lamp, who but ignites *hope* back to *all* lost and stranded *souls*."

Quotation #115

"*Innocence* is silent, never speaks *herself*. The *future* becomes *her* friend and *speaks* in volume for *her*."

Quotation #116

"*Life* is a lesson
learned after
crossing over time,
though not *for*
today, but
always for
tomorrow."

Quotation #117

"*When* life gives you nothing, *do* not *sit* back. Give *her* all you have and *watch* how she *learns* to give *back*."

Quotation #118

"*Today*, I, the human, shall *hold* on to the hands of *humanity* as she *takes* us onto the *bridge* of *mercy*."

Quotation #119

"*All* the impossible is made *possible through* the *invisible* bridge of *miracles*."

Quotation #120

"*Miracles* arrive within the *invisible coach*, called the *believers.*"

Quotation #121

"*Sacrifice* is the gift
of the *giver*.
For *within* this
journey, all is
but *achieved*."

Quotation #122

"*Storms* called
sorrows brewing in
the oceans of the
inner soul have
no place of warning,
but with time
as her friend,
she shall overcome
all the *obstacles*."

Quotation #123

"*Time* is but a *friend* for the truly *beloved*, for even *when* time *passes* by them, she *carries* their *tales* throughout *time*."

Quotation #124

"*Forgiveness* is but not a *gift given*, but a gift *achieved* throughout *eternity*."

Quotation #125

"*Know* even amongst the *tears* after the dark clouds, the *sun* is always out *there*."

Quotation #126

"*As* the sun rises
in the vast sky,
he beacons the
glory of hope
throughout the lands.
The windows open
allowing the sun to
pour in his glory
through to all the
creation near
and *afar*."

Quotation #127

"*Words* are just that, just words, *until* they *travel* time and become *words of* wisdom, for *wisdom* is an *age-old* virtue *acquired* through *time*."

Quotation #128

"*Life* is a miracle filled with wisdom, courage, and disappointment. Let all the achievements, positive or negative, guide you towards your goal. Hold on to the dreams and hope as you walk *forward.*"

Quotation #129

"*Yes*, there will be hurdles on your path as she is our companion of life. Remind yourself during all the storms of life, there is always hope our other companion of life. Keep her alive as she will guide all towards *victory*."

Quotation #130

"*Life* is a journey where we have all different companions walking alongside us. Let us take upon this journey, the blessings of hope. For holding on to the hands of hope, we shall reach our destination in *peace*."

Quotation #131

"*Words* gathered from history *create* the *future* for all *seeking* to learn from the *path* of *wisdom*."

Quotation #132

"*Life* is a sacred journey *filled* with *hurdles* and obstacles. Walk *across* this path *with* honor, dignity, and *courage* as our *spiritual companion.*"

Quotation #133

"*All* throughout the dark nights, *wait* and be *patient* for dawn approaches as *you* but *complete* this *journey* with complete *faith*."

Quotation #134

"*Miracles* are but the complete *faith* of the seeker. *Seek* her as she *awaits* upon your *door* to be *welcomed*."

Quotation #135

"*Disappointment* is but a *sacred* feeling we *walk* with, *for* it is the sole *reason* we but welcome *victory*."

Quotation #136

"*The* teacher and the student *walk* upon the same *path*. The only *difference between* them, *one* is but the past and one is but *the future*."

"*When* failure but *knocks* upon our *door*, it is only then we *open* our door to *victory*."

Quotation #138

"*Dreams* are born from within the *soul* seeking *peace*, blessings, *and* mercy. *Awaken* and *spread* peace, *blessings*, and mercy amongst *all*."

Quotation #139

"*Life* brings pain and joy upon our *boat* as we *take* the spiritual *journey* through this *ocean* of life, always *praying* for the *lighthouse* to guide *us*."

Quotation #140

ABOUT THE AUTHOR

I am an unknown person who lived the struggles, overcame the obstacles, as I have endured the pain and joy of life as they landed upon my door.

I like to be the unknown face to whom all can relate. I want you to see your face in the mirror when you search for me, not mine. For if it is my face in the mirror, then my friend you see a stranger. The unknown face is there so you see only yourself, your struggles, your achievements as you cross the journey of life. I want to be the face of a white, black, and brown, as well as the love we are always searching eternally for. If this world would have allowed, I would have distributed this inspirational quotation book to you with my own hands as a gift from a friend. Please take this book as a message from a friend.

You have my name and know I will always be there for anyone who seeks me. You can follow me @AnnahMariahRuby on Twitter, Ann Marie on my personal Facebook profile where the username is /annah.mariah.735, @TheAnnMarieRuby on my Facebook page, ann_marie_ruby on Instagram, and @TheAnnMarieRuby on Pinterest.

For more information about any one of my books, please visit my website www.annmarieruby.com.

I have published four books of original inspirational quotations:

Spiritual Travelers: Life's Journey From The Past To The Present For The Future

Spiritual Messages: From A Bottle

Spiritual Journey: Life's Eternal Blessings

Spiritual Inspirations: Sacred Words Of Wisdom

For all of you whom have requested my complete inspirational quotations, now I have for all of you, my complete ark of inspiration, I but call:

> *Spiritual Ark: The Enchanted Journey Of Timeless Quotations.*

I have also published a book of original prayers:

> *Spiritual Songs: Letters From My Chest.*

I am blessed to also share with you information about my upcoming book:

> *Spiritual Lighthouse: The Dream Diaries Of Ann Marie Ruby.*

I give you a sample from my prayer book, *Spiritual Songs: Letters From My Chest* as I have written this book of prayers from my heart for all of whom seek the spiritual journey.

FOREVER I AM YOURS

Oh my Lord, forgive me, guide me,

Protect me, bless me.

Oh my Lord, all around, I see only You.

All around, I feel is but Your love.

I but feel the immense power of Your guidance.

I ask of Your protection.

I seek for Your blessings.

All around I know my Lord but surrounds me.

Even amongst oceans of sin,

I find my Lord but guides.

All around the sinful ocean,

I find boats floating with my Lord's love.

Where people find sins but polluting the air,

I find my Lord's love but fills the blue sky.

The clouds pass by blessing me,

Washing my feet, hands, and my hair

From the basin of Heaven.

Blessed be as my Lord's blessings

Pour all over me.

My Lord, I but am in immense love.

I am but in deep meditation.

I am but Your true devotee.

I wish to spread this love and devotion

Amongst the creation.

As I talk with You, they call me crazy.

As I sit and fall to the ground in Your devotion,

They call me a liar.

As I walk miles after miles

Preaching Your truth, Your words,

They shout, throw their rocks,

Their words, their stones at me,

Trying to prevent me from preaching Your words.

They throw me off the cliffs.

They try to stop me for confused they are

And they try to confuse all.

They follow what is their ritual,

Their understanding given to them

By their forefathers.

Oh my Lord.

Oh my Lord.

Oh my Lord,

They but listen to a human.

They listen to the words of a human,

But they don't listen to the words of my Lord.

Oh my Lord, what am I to do.

I see the path and the way for the immense love

You have spread from Heavens above to the Earth.

I shall love them even when they hate me.

I shall guide them even when they want to be lost.

I shall teach them,

Even when they wish not to be taught,

For I shall walk with my head held up high,

Preaching Your words amongst all the creation,

For I know it is but they who are but lost,

For I have found You.

I have found Your Path.

I have been guided by You, my Lord.

I shall not fall prey amongst the sinners,

For I shall fall for them,

Teaching them the truth.

With their stones,

They shall try to change my words.

But death be calm, death be gentle

For even with death, I shall teach Your words,

For I know my Lord is there.

I know my Lord stands above the hill,

Hands held up for all of creation to return Home.

I, Your devotee, shall guide them

As I have found You.

This love I have found is my protection.

This love I have found is my guide.

This love I have found is my way.

And this love I have found is the music

From the flute of my heart.

For as I shall play the tunes on the flute,

I shall sing Your songs of love,

For I know Your devotees,

Your creation shall follow,

For they may not take my word,

Follow my path, or listen to this devotee,

But Your words, Your Path, and Your songs

Played on my flute shall reach them

For they are Yours, Your creation.

Oh my Lord,

As all the children of the world but return Home,

They shall repeat this tune I shall play

And leave behind for them to recite,

FOREVER I AM

YOURS.

*From my prayer book, *Spiritual Songs: Letters From My Chest*.

My Spiritual Collection

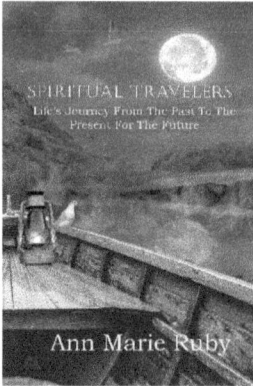

Spiritual Travelers:
Life's Journey From
The Past To The Present
For The Future

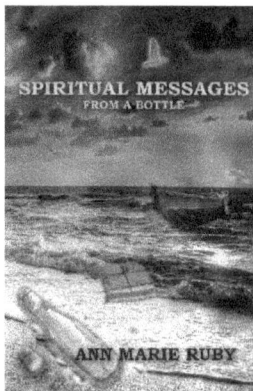

Spiritual Messages:
From A Bottle

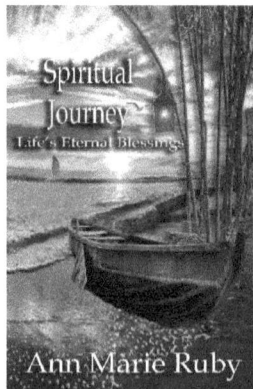

Spiritual Journey:
Life's Eternal Blessings

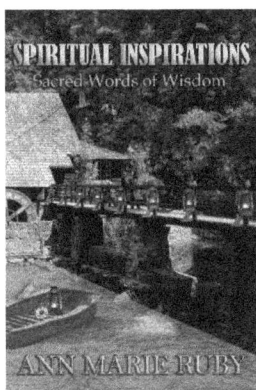

Spiritual Inspirations:
Sacred Words Of
Wisdom

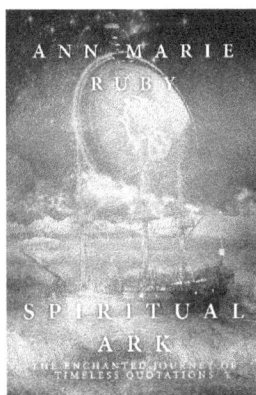

Spiritual Ark:
The Enchanted
Journey Of Timeless
Quotations

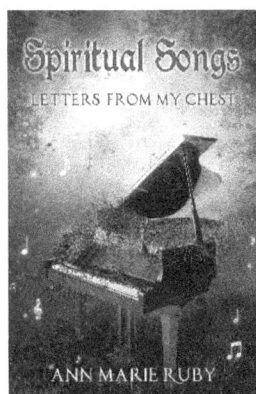

Spiritual Songs:
Letters From My Chest

My Upcoming Book

Spiritual Lighthouse:
The Dream Diaries Of Ann Marie Ruby

Within the dark, starless, foggy nights, my dreams appeared like the lighthouse always guiding me throughout my life. Dreams are spiritual guidance from the unknown. When the human body but falls asleep, it is then that our spiritual soul guides us throughout eternity. The soul walks into a parallel world where the past and the future exist in the same universe. Walk with me, as my soul but has walked the past and the future all throughout my life. Warnings, dangers, and surprises came upon my door, always guiding me like a lighthouse blinking in the dark night's sky. Alone, lost, and stranded I was until a lighthouse appeared within the ocean of the lost, my blessed dreams.

Take my hands and walk with me along this very personal path, as we journey together through my dream diaries, I call her, *Spiritual Lighthouse: The Dream Diaries Of Ann Marie Ruby*.

"Dreams are given from the Heavens above onto all within
the Earth beneath for within them lie the miracles of
eternity."

www.ingramcontent.com/pod-product-compliance
Lightning Source LLC
Chambersburg PA
CBHW021341290326
41933CB00037B/328